THE NIGHT THE SKY TURNED RED

GREAT PORTLAND MAINE FIRE OF JULY 4, 1866, AS TOLD BY THOSE WHO LIVED THROUGH IT

BY ALLAN M. LEVINSKY

COMMONWEALTH EDITIONS
AN IMPRINT OF APPLEWOOD BOOKS
CARLISLE, MASSACHUSETTS

DEDICATION

This book is dedicated, with much love, to my two grandchildren,
Vaughn and Isabelle Levinsky, who inspire me to write history
so that they will always know what went on in
their home city long before they arrived.

Published by Commonwealth Editions
an imprint of Applewood Books
Carlisle, Massachusetts 01741
www.commonwealtheditions.com

Commonwealth Editions publishes books about the history, traditions, and beauty
of places in New England and throughout America for adults and children.

To request a free copy of our current catalog
featuring our best-selling books, write to:
Applewood Books
P.O. Box 27
Carlisle, MA 01741

Manufactured in the United States of America

SPECIAL THANKS

One man, living at the time of the great Portland conflagration, has, because of his writings, been largely responsible for more than an abundant amount of information regarding the subject you are about to read. John Neal, born on Free Street in Portland in 1793 of Quaker parents, earned his living in many ways. He was a lawyer, an author, a literary critic, and a businessman. His writing, however, is what I am the most thankful for because his published account of the fire with all its minute detail helped me with my effort considerably. A short month after the blaze Neal's work was out on the streets of Portland. And because of his efforts, my efforts were made shorter. He had dug deeply into the experiences of Portland residents during the fire, giving us an idea of what their lives were like during that terrifying couple of days. For his efforts, I am grateful. Finding individual stories of Portland residents on July 4 and 5, 1866, would have been a Herculean task without John Neal's efforts.

This work is comprised of much information from Neal's work as well as newspapers from throughout the country, magazines, private letters, etc. Black-and-white fire photos are courtesy of the Maine Historic Preservation Commission, as are the photos of John Neal and John Marshall Brown. The Maine Historical Society provided the front cover fire photo and the fire map, and Judie Percival provided the other color fire photo.

AML
January 2014

ACKNOWLEDGMENTS

This book could not have been written without the help and encouragement of many people. First, my thanks go to my fellow employees of the Maine Historical Society who kept reminding me that I was supposed to write this book as I procrastinated on and on. When I finally realized they were right and finally picked up my pen and began, I discovered that I was going to need plenty of help in my research efforts. At the front of the line of volunteers was John Babin, whose efforts were monumental and who gave me the time I needed to do even more research. I am in his debt. Kathy Amoroso of the MHS digital department was always there with advice and help when I needed it. I am extremely grateful to Maine State Historian Earle G. Shettleworth Jr. who, as usual when called upon, was quick to offer his help.

And to those who read this account, I hope it will give you a greater understanding of what went through the minds of some of the residents who lived through this greatest urban fire disaster ever in the United States up to that date in history as you experience, through them, the terror and fear they felt as flames surrounded them.

Last, but not least, my wife, Sandra, deserves bushels of thanks for putting up with my postponing of many everyday chores with the excuse, "I'll do it tomorrow." Guess what? Tomorrow is here.

TABLE OF CONTENTS

FOREWORD

Catastrophic fires were a constant threat to nineteenth-century American cities and towns. Growth often took place so quickly that unregulated construction, the lack of central water supplies, and inadequate firefighting equipment left communities defenseless when fire struck. Two memorable New England fires occurred in Portsmouth, New Hampshire, in 1802 and Newburyport, Massachusetts, in 1811, leveling 132 and 250 buildings, respectively. In Maine, Bath lost its business district to fire in 1837, Rockland in 1853, and Augusta and Belfast in 1865. Yet none of these disasters approached the magnitude of the conflagration Portland suffered on July 4–5, 1866, a fire that left 10,000 people, one-third of the city's population, homeless and caused $12 million in damage. Portland's Great Fire of 1866 was the worst urban fire up to its time in American history, soon to be surpassed by Chicago in 1871.

Within the span of a day, Portland was transformed from Longfellow's "beautiful town that is seated by the sea," a place of shaded streets and frame houses, into a smoldering ruin that reminded the poet of Pompeii. But with their motto of *Resurgam* ("I will rise again."), Portlanders recalled with pride their recovery from two destructions in the seventeenth-century French and Indian War and a third on the eve of the American Revolution. From out of the ruins rose a city of broader and straighter streets lined with brick and stone Victorian commercial blocks, public buildings, churches, and houses. The community was made safer and healthier by water piped from Sebago Lake and more attractive by clearly defined commercial, industrial, and residential areas. In particular, home construction spread eastward to Munjoy Hill and westward to Deering Street, Parkside, and the Western Promenade, reaching the limits of the peninsula by 1900.

The Great Fire has always loomed large in the collective memory of the city. In the immediate aftermath, two of its most prominent citizens, John Neal and William Willis, wrote detailed histories of the event, Neal's appearing in booklet form and Willis's as a special issue of the *Portland Transcript*. On the 100th anniversary of the fire in 1966, the *Portland Evening Express* issued "The Day Portland Burned," an illustrated anniversary edition which I authored as a seventeen-year-old high school senior. More recently, in 2010, Michael Daicy and Don Whitney published *Portland's Greatest Conflagration: The 1866 Fire Disaster*.

Now, drawing heavily on period accounts of the fire, Allan M. Levinsky has produced *The Night the Sky Turned Red: The Story of the Great Portland Fire of July 4, 1866, as Told by Those Who Lived Through It*. Levinsky has written an engaging narrative of the fire, enriched by the immediacy of the words of eyewitnesses to the terrible event. To these firsthand descriptions he has added many photographic illustrations, primarily the work of the photographers who recorded scenes of the city in ruins: Soule and Whipple from Boston, Towle from Lowell, Moseley from Newburyport, and Sawyer from Bangor. No previous publication has reproduced so many period photographs of the destruction. These attributes alone make Levinsky's history a valuable addition to the nearly century and a half of literature on the Great Portland Fire of 1866.

—EARLE G. SHETTLEWORTH JR.
MAINE STATE HISTORIAN

PROLOGUE
THE RISE OF A CITY

I t all began in 1632. Two men and their families landed on what is now the eastern end of the Portland peninsula, found a suitable piece of land next to a stream of pure water at what is now Fore and Hancock Streets, and decided that this was a good place to build a homestead. George Cleeve and his partner Richard Tucker became the first white settlers of Falmouth Neck, now Portland.

By 1645 more settlers had found their way to the peninsula, and the population jumped to 40. Within a dozen years Massachusetts realized the potential of the area and annexed the vast territory, claiming jurisdiction over the province of Maine.

Population continued to grow, but the Native American residents had grown wary of the intruders claiming ownership of their land and hunting the game that fed them. In a number of attacks against the settlers, they eventually drove them away. By 1690 many of the former peninsula residents returned to the neck and resettled.

In 1718 the Massachusetts General Court reincorporated Falmouth and streets were laid out. The town continued growing until 1775, when a British fleet of five vessels, under the command of Lieutenant Henry Mowatt, destroyed the town with a day-long barrage of cannon fire that blew up or burned just about every building. This act became one of the deciding factors leading to the separation of this country from England.

By 1830 the population had grown to nearly thirteen thousand inhabitants. However, it was not until 1846 when a new era of prosperity would come to Portland. On July 4 of that year ground was broken for the construction of the Atlantic and St. Lawrence Railroad, which would become the city's link to Montreal, Canada, opening up great opportunities for the growth of both the city and population and open the way to the grain-producing areas of not only Canada but the western United States. Because Portland was the closest port to Europe, it became Canada's winter port when the St. Lawrence River froze over.

Track work was completed in 1853, and with the arrival of the railroads Portland became the railroad capital of Maine.

With the coming of steamships, regular schedules were begun between Portland and Boston and New York. It was not long before trans-Atlantic service was started.

With railroads and steamships operating, it was inevitable that business would grow, and soon large companies were building new buildings and starting new enterprises.

One of the biggest boons to business growth was the construction of a new and larger waterfront. Until 1853, when what would be called Commercial Street was completed, the waterfront was narrow, winding Fore Street. It was lined with old wharves and the combination of old cramped business houses and dwellings that had grown too small to handle all the new business.

City fathers realized that something was needed that would provide railroad tracks and spurs to commercial buildings, and, more importantly, connect the trains from Canada to the railroads going south which were on the other end of the peninsula. They voted to build a new street, which they would name, very aptly, Commercial Street. The plans called for the new roadway to be one hundred feet wide and stretch from the foot of Munjoy Hill in the east to the bridge in the western end of the city.

Fortunately, there was an abundance of vacant land on Munjoy and Bramhall Hills at either end of the proposed new street to use as landfill material. Tracks were laid down the middle of the new street, with spurs leading to the buildings on either side. Commercial Street was more than a mile long and paved with cobblestones, lending itself to the coming of a great period of expansion and prosperity.

Beckett's tourist guide for 1853 wrote, "Portland is destined to figure as one of the large cities of the Union. Within a few years it has taken a new start."

As well as an impressive new street, many new buildings were built.

They included City Hall, the Natural History Society, the Customs House, Mechanics Hall, the Grand Trunk Railroad Station, and the Maine Hospital.

As well as impressive buildings, there were many impressive visitors. Among them were Horace Greeley, Ralph Waldo Emerson, William Lloyd Garrison. And, of course, Portland's own Henry Wadsworth Longfellow frequently came to town to visit with his family. Royalty also came to Portland as the Prince of Wales toured the city.

Portland continued to grow and prosper through the 1850s, but change was just around the corner. With the election of Abraham Lincoln in 1860, the storm clouds that had been swirling over the slavery issue began to turn darker until April 12, 1861, when the Civil War erupted in a flash of cannon fire and the bombardment of Fort Sumpter in the harbor of Charleston, South Carolina.

Portland's prosperity would continue, largely because of the need for supplies and manufactured goods. But the all-important shipping business would suffer, largely due to the attacks of Confederate raiders on Portland ships. In fact, in 1863, the U.S. Revenue Cutter *Caleb Cushing* was blown up in Portland Harbor by a group of Confederate raiders. And in all, the city would contribute more than 10 percent of its population to the army and navy as their share of the war effort.

After the signing of the Confederate surrender at Appomattox in April of 1865, normalcy began to replace the anxiety of the war years. Despite the debt incurred during the war, business in Portland was still active. Midway through the war, horse-drawn streetcars began rolling over the tracks in 1863, allowing residents access to various sections of the city where they found new ways to entertain themselves and their families.

Modernizing to meet the population's ever-growing needs, small wood and brick buildings and homes were being replaced by two- and three-story brick and stone buildings.

Exchange Street was the financial area, with offices, banks, brokerage houses, and auction rooms all located in brick buildings.

Congress Street was the home of City Hall, public buildings, and churches as well as some manufacturing companies. The residential section lay west of Monument Square.

Noted Portland historian William Willis remarked in 1859 that "the city itself, rising roof above roof, interspersed with its steeples, towers, cupolas, and forest trees, as seen on entering the harbor by the ship channel, presents an imposing and beautiful appearance, suggestive of a place thrice its actual extent."

Now, with peace restored, Portlanders looked forward to the promise of a flourishing future. It was a time of reflection on the events of the previous twenty years, and the visions of what a bright future their hometown could provide them in the years ahead.

The *Portland Transcript* on June 30, 1866, wrote "What we wish to call attention to is the beauty of our city, its streets, its gardens, its situations, and surrounding scenery. No Portlander can at this season walk out streets in the twilight hours without being proud…"

Hopefully they would keep that beautiful picture in their minds, because a week later the Fates would fall on them like the executioner's ax and their lives would be changed in ways they could hardly imagine.

CHAPTER ONE
BIRTHDAY CELEBRATION

The Fourth of July holiday was a time for good fun and celebration for all the citizens of Portland and indeed the rest of the country. It was, after all, the birthday of the nation, and now in 1866 it would be the first time in six years that Americans, especially northerners, would have no war worries. It was a time to put their thoughts of the previous heart-wrenching war years aside. It would be a celebration of a new beginning with all the good things the future would bring.

For many weeks various committees had worked hard planning events for the special holiday that would make 1866 a year to remember and the first Independence Day that many Portland families would have their loved ones back from the terrible period that had just passed.

The *Portland Daily Press* in an article on July 2 wrote, "The arrangements for the celebration of the Fourth of July in the city are of such a character as will prove attractive to our friends from the country, who, generally on that day desire to visit the city, especially if there are to be exhibitions worthy of note."

The plans included many ways to ensure that the crowds would be large and that local businesses would share in the monetary rewards.

Even the weather continued to cooperate. As historian William Willis noted in his journal: "July 1—the air cool and pleasant—59–76. July 2nd—a beautiful day—61–80. July 3rd—a fine day. Cool morning and evening—65–79. July 4th—a very pleasant day—62–76."

Even the railroads contributed by scheduling special trains to pick up passengers who desired to get to Portland for all the fun and excitement.

Newspaper ads were placed in local papers announcing schedules. The *Portland Daily Press* wrote, "Special trains will be run over the Grand Trunk Road as far as Paris (Maine), by which visitors can arrive here soon after ten o'clock in the morning and leave after the exhibition of the fireworks in the evening. On the P.S& P. road (Portsmouth, Saco, and Portland Railroad) a train will go out to Biddeford after the fireworks are over. These trains run at one fair [sic] for the round trip. On the Portland and Rochester road, trains will run several times during the day, and one will leave in the evening after the exhibition is over."

The celebration actually began the Sunday before the Fourth. Out-of-town visitors began pouring into Portland, crowding the hotels and boarding houses. In a bit of self-promotion, the city was proclaiming in the *Portland Argus* that "this year's celebration promises to better than Boston's."

The crowds were enlarged in other ways. Because Portland was a terminal port for many cargo ships, it was also a liberty port for many sailors who came ashore to forget shipboard discipline and have a good time.

The locals themselves were also preparing for the exciting event to come. Store clerks were patriotically putting up red, white, and blue bunting on shop fronts while others were hanging streamers from the upper floors of higher buildings. Carpenters were putting the finishing touches on the reviewing stand in Congress Square at the intersection of High and Congress Streets. Most merchants were doing a booming business, as many of the visitors had come to shop in Portland stores, the most modern north of Boston.

One of the booming business enterprises that holiday week was the sale of fireworks to both visitors and locals. Everyone, it seemed, was preparing to put on their own fireworks displays.

The city's streets were also lined with the stands of competing peddlers, all trying to get their share of the visitor's money as they walked along the crowded thoroughfares. These temporary businessmen were offering a sundry array of tempting goods like ice cream, India rubber balloons, candy, and twitter-birds on a long wooden stick that vocalized and flapped their wings when the stick was waved through the air.

The selling scene changed at night to Market Square (now Monument Square). There, handcarts were set up and peddlers offered more-expensive items like watches and gold-colored watch fobs as well as celluloid shirt collars and other tempting items.

The square was lit by flickering flames from torches set above the wagons, and the air was filled with the competing shouts of the merchants, each valiantly trying to outdo their competition in the attempt to get the crowd's money.

Portland had an ordinance prohibiting this kind of activity, but on this occasion it was not enforced. For the Fourth of July holiday period most everything within reason was allowed. On Tuesday, July 3, the tempo increased as a huge contingent of new visitors arrived in Portland and checked into the city's hotels, like the Preble House and the United States Hotel, both in Market Square, and others like the American, the Commercial, and the International.

Every time someone picked up a newspaper they were bombarded with enticing advertisements describing what the efforts of the holiday planning committee's hard work had brought to fruition. One *Portland Daily Press* advertisement announced, "The committee of Arrangements for the celebration of the approaching Fourth of July, announces the following program as the order of the day. Salutes will be fired and the bells rung for one hour each, commencing at sunrise and at sunset."

More information appeared in the article on the day's plans.

"The Fantastics will appear this year in a stronger body than ever, and will commence their march between eight and nine o'clock in the morning making a grand display of oddities, caricatures and grotesque groupings and marching through the principal streets of the city which will produce the most laughable display which has ever been seen in Portland. During the forenoon there will be an old fashioned military training. This will be a sight worth seeing.

"At twelve o'clock the grand balloon ascension will be made by Messers Starkweather & Sever, from the Deering pasture. A grand opportunity will be afforded the tens of thousands to witness the process of inflating the balloon and of seeing the ascension."

William Willis wrote in a July 4 journal entry, "The fantastics looked too ridiculous for amusement, the balloon was a failure having burst into flames."

There were also more-mundane entertainments available to please the crowds. In the afternoon there was a baseball game scheduled to be held on the grounds of the Rolling Mills Co., formerly Camp Berry, between the Portland and Boston teams. If you were a betting man there was even something to hold your attention. The *Portland Daily Press* of July 2 described it as "a grand trotting match." To make it more exciting, there would be a purse of $250.00. The race, held at the Forest City Trotting Park, was scheduled for three o'clock in the afternoon. The newspaper article continued, "Some of the best horses in the state have been entered. There are seven entries, most of which have made their mile in less than 2:40. Among them are 'Dashaway'…a splendid trotting horse named 'Walter' from Calais, and other fast nags owned in this vicinity, among which is 'Portland Boy,' an untried animal but a great favorite. Two of the fast horses owned in distant parts of the state were too late in being entered."

So there were enough activities to keep everyone busy. Over in Market Square, at Deering Hall, the Trowbridge Minstrels and Pantomimes as well as the Morris Brothers were all hoping to sell out the house.

Not everything went smoothly. For unknown reasons, the gas supply that lit up the stores of the city's merchants had somehow cut off, throwing everyone in the dark. But not for long. Candles were lit for the evening's business activities and customers kept buying, keeping the merchants in a gay mood because of the day's excellent business.

Fireworks dealers had done a banner business and most had sold out their stock of incendiaries. All day and night before the Fourth, there had been a steady cacophony of explosions, everything from small pops to ground-shattering explosions of the more-powerful firecrackers.

By Tuesday evening July 3, the city was a bedlam of sound and the air was filled with smoke from small bonfires lit in empty spaces and at backyard parties all over Portland.

Perhaps one of the most anticipated events was the coming of the circus, aptly named G.F. Bailey & Co.'s Great Quadruple Combination. They arrived on Monday night, July 2, and the personnel worked through the night setting up their tents. Early on Tuesday morning they were ready for business. The circus had unloaded their train on Commercial Street and set up on the Western Promenade near Arsenal Street.

By ten in the morning of July 3, Portland's streets were lined with thousands of spectators from Pine to Congress and Middle to watch the grand procession of colorful wagons and animals and circus acts. All this hoopla was designed to entice the viewers to come see the great show that afternoon and evening and the two performances on the Fourth. The star attraction was a huge hippopotamus in a cage drawn by four elephants, a sight never before seen in Maine. According to the ads in the papers, the hippo was imported by the circus at a cost of sixty thousand dollars, an immense sum at that time.

The procession was accompanied by Professor Whittier's Metropolitan Opera Band, loud enough to make many watchers clap their hands over their ears in self-protection.

The circus owner, Mr. G.F. Bailey, was not part of the Bailey family of the Barnum and Bailey Circus we know today.

All of the hype and advertising seemed to have paid off, as the Tuesday afternoon and evening as well as the Wednesday afternoon and evening performances were all sold out. In short, there was enough activity to engage everybody's attention from early morning until late at night.

Of course, the most anticipated event was yet to come. It was the one that always attracts extremely large crowds and draws the loudest oohs and aahs. It was, of course, the fireworks exhibition.

Portland officials promised the event to be "the most brilliant ever exhibited in the state." According to the *Portland Daily Press*, "It will take place in Deering Pasture which is the best place in the city for such a purpose, as the rising grounds afford everyone an opportunity to witness the display and be without the reach of danger."

Little could the multitude of residents and visitors realize what was in store for them later on that fateful July Fourth day that would affect their lives for years to come and place them so close to being grasped by the hands of danger.

CHAPTER TWO
SOUND THE ALARM

t was 4:14 on the afternoon of July Fourth and the celebration was progressing. Some of the planned events had gone well, some not so successfully. William W. Ruby, one of Portland's black citizens, was approaching the corner of Commercial and Maple Streets when he spotted something that did not look right: A small fire had broken out in a pile of wood shavings in the yard of a boatyard and had begun to follow a course through the stream of wood scraps toward a planning mill.

Ruby immediately began raising the alarm, shouting in a loud voice that there was a fire in District Eight. He was familiar with the district because he had many friends in Portland's fire companies.

Ruby was Portland-born in 1834 but moved to New York City with his parents when he was five years old. According to the book *Maine's Visible Black History*, by H.H. Price and Gerald E. Talbot,

> "During his eleven years in the big city, he was selected for an exclusive honor in a fire company...during the daylight hours the chief could read the company number on the engines as they approached the scene; at night, however, it was impossible to determine the nine converging units.
>
> "The practice was for each fire company to have a torch boy. This was a lad of about twelve years of age, selected by the company, whose duty it was to respond on all night alarms, light the torch bearing the etched numbers on the glass lens, and run a block ahead of his company. The chief recognized the illuminated

whale oil torches leading the engines and assigned each company accordingly. Hundreds of boys in each city would want to hold this prestigious position, but only one per company was permitted. This was the honored position for which William Ruby was chosen in a New York engine company."

William Ruby moved back to Portland when he was sixteen and maintained his association with the Portland Fire Department, making many friends among the firefighters. He was even seen running to fires along with his firemen friends.

On that fateful Fourth of July in 1866, Ruby's alarm was probably the first given. His cry was quickly picked up by others from street to street and ultimately by the bells in the churches, one after another; then the alarm was picked up by the fire companies.

William Ruby's interest in the firefighting profession never waned. According to *Maine's Visible Black History*, "In 1884 William Ruby was accepted as a member of Steam Fire Engine Machigonne 1, one of the busiest engine companies in the state. This was a paid position. Members received pay for each alarm to which they responded. He was appointed as a Pipeman, the envied position of controlling the nozzle of the hose line. Many firemen were company members for years without holding this position. In two years, the members of the engine company elected Ruby as captain of the company. In 1888 he was promoted to assistant engineer. There were only four assistant engineers, now known as deputy chiefs, under the chief engineer. This was a highly respected position in the view of both firefighters and civilians—a city position of authority."

Even after retirement, William Ruby's interest in firefighting and the fire department remained, and he answered the alarm for many major fires in Portland. Because of his experience and vast knowledge, he was allowed to participate and was assigned a position by the fire chief.

CHAPTER THREE
THE FATE OF A YOUNG BOY

Wednesday July 4, 1866, dawned giving every indication that it would be an extremely pleasant day for all the anticipated activities that were planned to entertain Portland's citizens. William Willis noted in his journal that the low for the morning was a relatively mild sixty-two degrees and later reached a high near eighty.

One of the city's residents whose life would be greatly affected on this day was a youth of sixteen named Cyrus H.K. Curtis, whose name in later life would become famous in the publishing world and to the public. He had always looked forward to this particular holiday with its parades and all the other exciting activities, especially the fireworks. Most of all, he shivered with excitement at the thought of his opportunity to blow off some of his own miniexplosives. In fact, the need for ready cash to purchase these precious items was responsible for his first job four years earlier in 1862.

Edward W. Bok, who would become, years later, the son-in law of Curtis, wrote a biography of him in 1923 titled *The Man From Maine*. He tells how Curtis, at the age of twelve, earned his first wages.

"Now, the Fourth of July is a very long day in a boy's calendar, for it begins early and ends as late as he can make it last. And it follows usually that a few pennies are not likely to last too long over such a day. It was in this predicament that this twelve year old boy found himself on the Fourth of July 1862 when, at five o'clock, he banged into his mother's home, his mind full of evening plans, and asked for 'a little change'! He had evidently forgotten that his mother had already given him some 'change' in the morning…

"'If you want money to spend,' she suggested, 'why not go out and earn it?'…and then and there, at the age of twelve, the first dawning consciousness of the business career of Cyrus Herman Kotzschmar Curtis broke upon him."

After a short period of contemplation, he finally asked his mother, "'If I earn some money can I keep it all for myself and spend it on what I want?'" His mother agreed. When Cyrus hit the street he contemplated ways to earn his daily allowance.

A short time later he met a friend who didn't appear to be too happy. He had been on the street selling newspapers and still had three copies of the *Courier* under his arm that nobody had seemed willing to buy.

Curtis thought this looked like an opportunity and offered his friend his last remaining three cents for them. It took three hours for Cyrus to finally sell the papers but he had tripled his money, even though it was now too late to take part in any Fourth of July activities, so he went home.

The next day he went to the *Courier* office and purchased more papers and doubled his money. As time went by, things grew difficult. Competition among the newsboy clan was very keen and each one had his own territory. Because Cyrus was of small stature, he found he was more or less left out of the picture. Finally, he discovered that by taking papers by boat out to Fort Preble, the soldiers there eagerly took all his stock at a higher price for his trouble and he would then head happily for home.

Because of his success, other newspaper publishers sought him out, and Curtis found himself working winter and summer. He would get up at quarter to four, service his routes, have breakfast at seven and go to school at nine. He later said, "I liked the smell of papers and printing presses. I saved up some money and bought a small press and printed my own paper."

By 1866 the Curtis enterprise was going strong.

But on the Fourth of July he experienced another turning point in his life. Late in the afternoon he heard the fire bells ringing and along with some of his friends ran looking for the fire.

Edward Bok, in his biography, describes what happened next. "It was fully two miles away from his house, and when he got there it had gained great headway. He heard people say that the entire block where the fire started was doomed. The boy stayed as long as he could then left for supper." When he finally arrived home he found his mother packing some of her valuable possessions. He informed her of the fire's location and that in his opinion the blaze would never reach their home as it was over two miles away. Bok continues,

"The mother argued, with Yankee shrewdness, that foresight was always better than hindsight, and after a light supper she began to pack again. The father was away from home for the night in a neighboring city, and so the boy was told by his mother that he would be her sole reliance in saving what they could. He had a sister, five years younger, and what an eleven year old girl could do she did.

"The fire had been devouring block after block, and the boy began to see that his mother was perhaps right in at least taking precautions. Every truck and moving vehicle in the neighborhood was already commissioned by the neighbors and so the only means of moving their possessions which the family could command was the boy's little express wagon. This he filled to the top with the articles most desirable of saving and, unaccustomed to such a load, the tiny wagon broke down so the three could only carry to what they deemed a place of safety, all that their arms could hold.

"It is shameful, but a fact, that there are always persons ready to take advantage of the helpless in times of stress. It proved so with the Curtis family. The mother had put all the most valuable belongings of the family in a sideboard, hoping to find some means of moving this one piece of furniture. While she was exploring the neighborhood for some means, she saw two men steal into the house and come out carrying the sideboard, the contents of which they had heard the mother describe. The source of initiative invariably present in the career of the son is found in the mother.

"She saw instantly that the most valuable of the family's possessions were in danger, but even amid all the nervous excitement of the moment, in the absence of anyone to counsel her, the mother made up her mind to turn what looked like a misfortune to her advantage. The sideboard was an old fashioned heavy one, and the men had difficulty in carrying it. The mother, however, walked behind them, at a safe distance, and when they carried it over two miles from her house to a point of assured safety, exactly where she had tried in vain to get someone to truck it, she accosted the men, claimed the property, and sent them running for their lives.

"At midnight the fire had reached the Curtis home on Wilmot St., laid it in ashes, and within a few hours afterward had travelled another mile and a half, more than fulfilling the mother's instinct and reducing the best part of the city of Portland to ruins.

"The mother and her son and daughter had found a temporary home beyond the fire zone, but there was no sleep for the active boy at such a time, and he remained up all night. In the early morning hours he ventured near his one-time home to see if anything was left of it, only to find his father standing at the foot of the street disconsolately gazing with his hands clasped, in the direction of the spot where a few hours before he had left his family and home. Desolation was all around him, and he had not the remotest idea whether his family was alive, or, if alive, where its members were. He had heard of the fire in the city where he had gone to spend the night and had returned to Portland on an early morning train. There the boy had found his stricken father.

"With his home burned down, his printing plant wiped out, with no insurance, the young Curtis faced life in all its grief. He was sixteen and had just finished his first year in high school. He decided he must leave school and devote all his time to making a livelihood. The days of boyhood were over."

After the fire, Cyrus Curtis moved to Boston and then to Philadelphia where he became a media mogul and a very wealthy man.

CHAPTER FOUR
THE SUGAR HOUSE MELTS

The fire alarm bells that young Cyrus Curtis heard around five o'clock in the afternoon of July Fourth, sending him and his friends in search of the fire, were actually sounded because of a blaze that started in the yard of Deguio's boat shop on Commercial Street near the corner of Maple Street.

There have been many theories speculating how the fire actually started. Some people guessed that the cause was sparks from a passing railroad engine landing on wood shavings in and around the boat shop. However, the most widely accepted cause is that a passing boy carelessly threw a firecracker onto shavings just outside the shop igniting dry wood shavings. From there the flames spread quickly to adjoining buildings.

The fire jumped across Commercial Street to a planing mill on York Street, then raced along that block to the J.B. Brown sugarhouse at Commercial, York and Maple Streets. The huge sugar refinery was an eight-story structure built in 1845 and expanded several years later. It employed 150 workers and produced 150 barrels of sugar each day. The 1856 *Portland City Directory* describes the sugarhouse as "one of the chief objects of business interest in our city, both from the magnitude of the buildings comprised under the name, and the extent of the works carried on within.

"The business is the manufacture of sugar from molasses imported from the West Indies. The sugars are remarkably clean and will otherwise compare favorably with the various styles of brown sugar in the market."

The amount of business done was probably near a half-million dollars a year in 1866 dollars. The business was started by John Bundy Brown, considered by many as Portland's outstanding citizen. He would go on to build the Falmouth Hotel, the city's largest and most luxurious, probably the equal to any hotel in Boston. Brown also developed a large section of the Western Promenade. He established J.B. Brown and Sons, a company that grew into one of the largest development companies east of Boston and is still in business and still family owned.

The sugarhouse was closed on July Fourth for the holiday, probably preventing what could have become a much greater disaster if it had been open and full of workers. The building was like a sitting duck as the flames approached due to the thousands of barrels and other flammable materials stored in it.

When the fire first started there was little concern. The Portland Fire Department had always in the past been highly capable of taking care of fires quickly and efficiently. Losses in previous years had been low, leaving the population in a lack of concern.

Portland's John Neal in his valuable *Account of the Great Conflagration*, published shortly after the fire, wrote, "Our losses for a long time had been so trifling, that although insurance rates were unreasonably low in comparison to rates elsewhere, very few of our people had more than a third or half insurance, while others by hundreds, had no insurance at all, and some few of our large property holders had been long in the habit of insuring themselves, or insuring in home offices with small capital upon the ground that all such business had better be kept at home—forgetting that if the principle were sound, next door neighbors might as well insure each other and the system of mutual guaranties against fire."

For the first half-hour or so after the ringing of the first alarm, nobody paid much attention to it. There was such a lack of concern among the thirty thousand residents of Portland that few took the trouble to find out what the danger really was. There were all kinds of stories circulating. Alarm bells stopped ringing and started again, each time a little louder and ringing with more vigor.

Portland residents knew that their fire department had always been capable of handling fires efficiently and quickly. Only a few weeks before, on a Saturday night, they had been called out when fire was discovered in the furniture manufacturing shop of Walter Corey located in the rear of Exchange Street. The four story building was brick and the fire was discovered on the second floor near the elevator. It took the firemen more than three hours to bring the flames under control. The building, owned by John Neal, was insured for two thousand dollars and was fully covered. Mr. Corey had sufficient insurance to cover his stock and equipment.

The *Daily Press* of June 18, 1866, gave great credit to the fire department for preventing what could very well have been a disaster as the buildings surrounding Mr. Corey's were all made of wood, and had the flames jumped to even one of them it could have led to a very bad situation.

The paper wrote, "Our firemen worked with a will. They were prompt at the alarm, and in a few moments the Falmouth (name of the fire engine) had a stream of water upon the fire, and the other steamers quickly followed. Fortunately the adjoining building to the one on fire had been bricked up on that side, and the gallant and persistent efforts of the department prevented the flames from torching the other buildings. The firemen deserve great credit for their efforts on this occasion.

"The value of steam fire engines was never before so apparent. Without them the whole of the south side of Exchange St., from Middle to Fore St., would have gone… Hand engines could have done nothing towards preventing the fire from spreading, for the power could not be brought upon them to have thrown the water the distance required."

After a while, a man riding along State Street stopped and told a group of people who were congregated on the street, that while he was over on Cape Elizabeth he had seen enough to satisfy him that the fire that started in the boat shop "would certainly take the great Sugar House of Brown and Sons."

Most of the people, however, were really not concerned about the fate of the giant sugarhouse. They mistakenly thought that the building had been constructed with such great care that it was more than likely fireproof. Besides, even though it occupied a high footprint it was completely walled in from the whole neighborhood. It was taken for granted that it was more than likely that there, if nowhere else, the fire would go out by itself. Because of this, no one was overly concerned or felt that people outside the immediate neighborhood should feel any alarm or anxiety.

John Neal wrote in his account of the fire, "But by and by the wind sprang up; a great roaring was heard afar off, and coming nearer and nearer—the door steps and house-tops began to be crowded with breathless listeners—all conversation was carried on in a low voice and consisted of little more than brief hurried questions and answers; the heavens gathered blackness, and a hurricane of fire swept over the city carrying cinders and blazing fragments of wood far into the country and actually firing houses on North Street, more than a mile away, and soon after in Falmouth, five miles distant."

The wind carried the fire, which ultimately spread out like a fan, with such speed that people all over the city began pouring water on their houses to try and keep them from catching fire. Confusion set in as residents did not know whether they should run or save as many of their prized possessions as they could carry.

It did not take long for a shortage of transportation to develop with so many people all having the same thoughts. Wagons became impossible to find. Children's little wagons were used when they became the only available transportation.

Nobody could find a safe place to move their belongings to and it was a continuing process of moving their valuable goods again and again. Fireproof warehouses with iron shutters and roofs of slate soon crumbled from the terrific heat and fell in heaps. Iron melted and metal signs turned to liquid and dropped to the ground. Kegs of nails were fused together into solid masses and glass and crockery became like crystal jewels, welded together from the terrible heat.

The blaze was fast moving, so it was not long before many streets were all on fire at the same time. The faster the flames moved and the more of the city that was kindled, the harder and stronger the wind blew, causing the flames to become even more intense. The scene was becoming more and more like Dante's Inferno.

It was not long before Portland's situation would deteriorate exponentially, from being a city on fire to a city immersed in a conflagration.

CHAPTER FIVE
THE CHIEF ENGINEER REPORTS

The chief engineer of the Portland Fire Department, Spencer Rogers, knew almost immediately that the city was in great danger. His experience told him that this fire was different. The weather conditions in 1866 were very dry and the buildings, heated by the sun and left dry by the lack of rain, were ready to kindle from just a spark of fire. And, operating the department's equipment was becoming troublesome.

The first engine that arrived on the scene, for some reason, would not take water. The second and third pieces of equipment that arrived lost much valuable time because the hoses began to burn. Before the fourth engine arrived, a second fire was reported on Union Street and that engine was dispatched to that location.

Engineer Rogers wrote, "It soon became evident to me that our fire department was inadequate to stop the fire. Appeals for help were telegraphed Lewiston, Gardiner, Bath, Biddeford, Hallowell, and Augusta. And a special train was sent to Saco. Before this relief could reach us, the fire was past control."

William Willis describes what happened in this journal entry: "Wednesday July 4th. Great fire. Fireworks were suspended by a real and most distinctive fire which began in a cooper's shop on Commercial Street near High and swept with great rapidity along Commercial, York, Fore, Middle, and at this writing is raging on Cotton and Cross Streets, threatening Union Street."

John Neal, in his published account of the greatest urban conflagration in the history of the United States, best tells of the terror and confusion of the residents. "Most of the streets…were all on fire at once and though the fire companies belonging to the city as well as others labored on, hour after hour, without quailing or flinching in the midst of danger as great as that of the battlefield—with falling chimneys and tumbling walls, and showers of broken slate, and clouds of smoke, and blazing cinders all about them, and a suffocating, scorching atmosphere that few could breathe in safety, they only succeeded in staying the conflagration along the outskirts; leaving the main current to exhaust itself, at a distance of more than a mile from where it originated—sweeping away most of our public buildings …and stopping only in one direction for lack of material; in another at a sand bank, and in another at the old graveyard (Eastern Cemetery at the foot of Munjoy Hill) and where an eye witness asserts that he saw a great multitude rushing hither and thither, like many distracted creatures, in the midst of rolling clouds and flashing fires, as if the sheeted sleepers had been scared back to life."

Neal goes on to compliment the local and assisting fire departments, giving them the highest praise for their work in spite of their own personal danger as they darted between the flaming buildings.

He continues his narrative, telling of the despair of the situation. "But from the first or within two hours it was seen that steamers and fire companies, however efficient, on all ordinary occasions, were entirely powerless. Water was of no use: it was instantly converted into flame, flashing up like gunpowder when it struck the glowing mass, and so fierce and terrible was the onset that many barely escaped with their lives while yet the danger was far off."

Neal describes the experience of one woman who told him of her ordeal. She said, "After spending hours in getting ready to move if it became necessary, my husband with one or two friends were carrying water up to the roof trying to keep it wet. I was suddenly called upon to flee for my life, even though the fire seemed far off. I had just enough time to escape with my two children, with my sister and her two children following. The air was already so hot it scorched my throat and I had to clap a handkerchief over my mouth and run for my life, leaving house and furniture and clothing to be consumed almost instantly."

Within five minutes after they left the house, which was located on India Street, it was engulfed in flames.

Neal describes how the fire affected him. "I myself had an office on Exchange Street, far out of the range of the fire. It was protected on both sides by brick walls, without a single opening, and on one side by a vacant lot. In the rear was a new brick building, only two stories high, and all the back windows were fortified with iron shutters. Three times I passed that way in the course of an hour or two, without an idea of being obliged to move my library and office furniture, and only at last consented to open my safe and take away a small basket of papers, owing to the urgent persuasion of my family—for I knew of no safe place even if I could have obtained a dray or carriage at any price. Within the next hour, that building, together with the whole of a large block of stores and offices running the whole length of Exchange Street to Middle Street, was a pile of ruins, and all the iron shutters they had put their trust in were shriveled like parchment, and fluttering like old clothes on the cross wires."

Meanwhile, many businessmen were trying to save their merchandise and records even though the fire was still over a quarter of a mile away from them. It wasn't long before drays and carts were impossible to locate.

There was a sudden change in the path of the fire as the wind picked up due to the increased intensity of the flames, and nature itself and soon a block of four and five story warehouses on Middle Street were in peril of burning.

Onlookers thought that the height and construction of the lofty buildings would surely stop the fire from spreading farther, but within five minutes the flames were surging through all the windows and, according to John Neal, "On came the fiery whirlwind; all the streets, lanes and alleys roaring like so many furnace flues, and within five minutes from the time the blast struck that iron clad building, which seemed to have been providentially left in its way, the flames were surging through all the windows, and reaching the Evans block, another new, handsome and lofty building on the opposite side off Middle Street, through which it passed in a few minutes without stopping, till it struck Mussey's Row, and uniting with currents of flame, driven by a strong wind through Plumb, Union and Cross Streets, burst upon the Barbour Block, the Fox Block, the post office and Custom House, and all the intermediate stores till it reached

Congress Street and broke over the new City Building, utterly destroying the whole, with the exception of the Custom House and post office, which built of granite and iron, and supposed to be perfectly fire-proof, will have to be taken down and wholly rebuilt."

Nobody expected the damage to great granite buildings like the Custom House, but all the stone flaked off and was transformed into shapeless, incandescent boulders and broken fragments, and the cornices and heavy projections smashed dangerously into the ground.

The conflagration raged on for fifteen hours before finally burning itself out. From the beginning, it followed the diagonal direction it started with, cutting across the most crowded and busiest parts of the city, blowing into the outskirts where it was occasionally checked and turned in new directions.

The lack of water from wells, cisterns, and reservoirs as well as a city-wide water system, made the fire department's job impossible. Attempts were made to block the flames from spreading by using explosives to blow up some buildings, creating what was hoped to be a fire block. Nothing worked until nature itself took over and there was nothing else to burn.

July 5 proved to be another hot day, with the temperature reaching the mideighties. William Willis turned to his journal, entering his impressions of the great fire. "The fire raged all night and was burning this morning. Among the last buildings destroyed were the new City Hall and a Free Street block at the foot of the street. The fire swept in a northerly direction diagonally across the city, taking all the northerly side of Fore Street from Centre to across India Street, all Middle, both sides from Free to Munjoy Hill, all Federal below Temple, Cross, Union, Silver, Wilmont and so on. Wood's Hotel and a dwelling opposite, six churches, 2nd and 3rd Parish, Universalist, Sweden, Catholic, St. Stephens, post office and Custom House, and all the banks and printing offices—my office, losing my furniture and many if not all of my books. Valuable papers were put in the safe but whether they are safe or not, time will disclose. 1500 families are rendered homeless and are seeking shelter. The citizens and the city have made temporary provisions for them and supplies have been sent in from Boston, Lewiston and other places—the local insurance companies will be ruined and how much will be obtained from the offices remains to be proved. The loss can be reached only by millions. The Athenium lost all its library and building, the register of deeds all his records of titles to the great dismay of all real estate owners."

The next day, July 6, Willis wrote, "The people are at work cleaning up the streets, Mr. Brown has sent men to work preparing to rebuild his sugarhouse. Other persons are making preparations. The records of deeds were not destroyed but those of the probate office were. The vaults of the Trailer's and 1st National Banks have been opened and the contents are entirely safe. Abundant supplies and provisions have been sent from Boston and New York and towns in this state. Large sums of money have also been contributed in Boston and New York, and the homeless people are comfortably provided for."

CHAPTER SIX
ANOTHER EYEWITNESS VIEW

The flames spread their destructive arms all through the night, turning the night sky red, and continued into the next morning, rushed along with the help of near-hurricane-force winds created by nature and the intensity of the fire itself. Portland resembled Dante's Inferno with renters and home owners desperately trying to save what they could of their possessions by moving them from one location to another in the hopes they could save as many earthly belongings as possible.

Transportation was nowhere to be found, as everything with wheels had already been taken by Portlanders who were taking no chances at the beginning of the fire. Whole families were seen running through the streets, their arms loaded with their most prized possessions. Some of the younger children trailed behind, their little red wagons loaded with precious goods. The heat was intense. Glowing embers were everywhere flying through the air like small meteorites before ultimately dropping everywhere—to the ground, the roofs of buildings, and onto the piles of possessions that had been left by other residents in the hopes they would be safe.

It was a losing battle. The fire that was expected to be out soon after it started burned on for fifteen hours, relentlessly heading diagonally across the most crowded and busiest section of Portland and the fringes of the outskirts until the wind changed direction and finally there was nothing more to burn.

Although the conflagration was for all intents and purposes extinguished, there was still much fear among both the government and the residents. Portland's mayor, Augustus Stevens, posted a notice proclaiming Look to the Fire. Watch Tonight! urging all the citizens who had not suffered the loss of their houses or stores to keep a sharp look out for any recurrence. He urged them to keep buckets and tubs filled with water handy and to keep their roofs "well wet" in case the winds changed, rekindling the fire and spreading it into the untouched western portion of the city.

The fear of a fast-spreading fire was not something to take lightly, as noted by an eyewitness to the 1866 fire. In a talk given at a social gathering and later reported in an article on October 13, 1929, in the *Portland Telegram*, Samuel Rumery, a well-known historian from the Maine Historical Society, was reminiscing about his early boyhood days. He ended his talk with a description of his experience on July 4, 1866, at the big fire. He was eleven years old at the time. It was toward the end of the day and Rumery and a companion had run out of fireworks. After a busy day of exciting activities, the boys decided to replenish their supply. After the purchase, Rumery and his buddy had just left Harlow's store at the corner of Union and Fore Streets when the church bells began ringing, sounding a fire alarm. When the boys reached Deguio and Dyer's boat shop there were still few spectators.

Rumery continued, "At that time, there was only a limited supply of water with which to fight a fire of any magnitude. As we boys ran around the front of the boat shop on Commercial Street we could see that the tide was pretty near at an ebb. My recollection is that the first engines drew their water from a cistern on Cotton Street, and by the time the first stream was turned on the fire, the boat shop was a mass of flames. A small lot of boards back of the boat house next caught fire. Then a planing mill fronting on York Street began to smoke along the edges of the roof and shortly afterwards flames shown through the windows, and as the building was filled with carpentry work, it was evident that the building and all its contents was doomed."

About this time, the southwest wind began to pick up noticeably in force, blowing sparks and charred brands onto the roofs of nearby buildings. The next important building in the path of the fire was the J. B. Brown Sugar House, which fronted Commercial Street. Hundreds of hogsheads of molasses were stored inside, waiting to be turned into sugar.

Rumery continued, "Mr. Brown, I believe, was the first man to realize that this was no ordinary fire to contend with and offered a dollar an hour to workmen to help move his books, papers, and other valuables. The offer was accepted and the moveable contents of his office were quickly brought out. The great building was soon after wrapped in flames."

Rumery became so engrossed in watching all that activity that he lost track of both time and his companion. By the time he got home, there was a glare over the horizon.

"My father asked me how far the fire was from our house and I told him the last building I saw burning was on Fore Street. Father then decided to move our household goods to the new Franklin Street factory. I was sent with a message…to the night manager of the factory and soon four men and two teams came and removed our belongings. Judge John H. Williams was the only neighbor that followed my father's example."

Realizing that they needed another team, one was acquired and was soon loaded with the remaining most valuable of their possessions and taken to the driveway next to the factory. "I was given the reins and was told that in case the fire should threaten the factory, to drive the load down onto Franklin wharf. This I did, and from that time until daylight my impressions of the fire were received at a considerable distance."

CHAPTER SEVEN
MR. STERLING'S ORDEAL

The notation in William Willis's journal noted that July 6 had dawned with the promise that it would be "a sultry day," and indeed it was as the temperature rose to the high eighties. Portland residents took advantage and set to cleaning the streets and their property of the vast amount of fire rubble. They were also desperately attempting to salvage any personal property that might have miraculously avoided the flames.

By now, the army had lent a vast number of tents to the city to provide shelter for those who were unable to find shelter with relatives or friends, and a tent city began to grow all the way to the top of Munjoy Hill and along the Eastern Promenade. Large and small communities across the country had run front-page stories on Portland's "great conflagration" and an effort to raise money to help the devastated city and its citizens overcome their difficulties had already begun to show results, with promises of funds to arrive soon.

Money was not the only relief beginning to arrive in Portland. Carloads of supplies and food also began coming in and soup kitchens were set up to feed the hungry. Although every tent sent to the city had been set up and occupied by Saturday, July 7, and every available house that had any room for guests had been filled with survivors, there were still nearly 6,000 persons who were without shelter.

An article in the July 10 *New York Times* noted, "The summary manner in which people were obligated to leave their homes… found them in houses, open fields, and in tents, barns and anywhere that offered them space to watch their little stock of goods. Some had saved a hoop skirt and a stove; others a tin dipper and a couple of chairs, a tea kettle and a pair of parlor pictures, a washstand and boots, and all such miscellaneous collections in small quantities. Pianos were numerous, and quite a number of families saved their piano and a cat. One man, worth in the morning over $50,000, pulled a pair of his wife's boots out of his pocket, and said it was all he had saved."

The food sent to feed the hungry was prepared and distributed at the old city hall on Market Square (now Monument Square). All day long men, women, and children of all ethnicities huddled together to eat and commiserate.

As in all disasters, along with the good came the bad, and Portland was no exception. The city filled with thieves and pickpockets from Boston, New York, and any place where those with criminal tendencies felt they would be able to profit at the expense of the less fortunate.

In its article, the *New York Times* continued, "It is a fact disgraceful to humanity that hundreds of desperadoes have arrived in the city for the worst of purposes… the further spoliation of the smitten community. The police force are worn out with their ceaseless toil by day and night, and unable to cope with any additional scoundrelism [sic], and every resident of the city is jaded with labor; but armed guards are posted at night at all places where any raid upon property is apprehended. General Hooker had been requested by telegraph by the city authorities to send a company of soldiers, and has responded in the affirmative. A body of Marines are also here from the navy-yard at Portsmouth, so that if there be a contest, the villains will meet a hot reception."

Because the fire had deprived Portland of its supply of gas for lighting, the nights were cloaked in the deepest darkness, a great benefit for those with evil on their minds like a man named Charles Sanborn, who had come to Portland from Parsonfield, Maine, specifically to benefit illegally. He was caught on Munjoy Hill trying to set fire to a house to create a new alarm that would draw people from their homes to help, leaving their own homes open to robbery by one Mr. Sanborn. He was promptly caught and lodged behind bars with many others of his kind.

Other examples of illegal activity included Moses Russel, who had his pocket picked on Congress Street of $1500; another man was robbed on Middle Street of $400 and a fireman was beaten by two roughs. Another incident was reported in the *Portland Transcript* that told of a man and his wife who had been burned out of their house and went over to Cape Elizabeth to board. When they were shown to their room, they discovered that it was furnished with their own furniture.

Portland's police department had duties other than catching bad guys during the conflagration. Many of them gave valuable aid helping the fire department fight the flames. One example was an ex-deputy marshal, a Mr. Sterling, who had actually resigned from the police force in the spring of 1866. As the fire gained headway he decided to lend a hand in helping the firemen when it became evident that they were in desperate need of all the help they could get. Mr. Sterling worked through the night and well into the next day. As he explained it, "Hustling in the heat and smoke and flying cinders until his clothes were burned as full of holes as a pepper box."

When the fire first broke out, Sterling made his way to Brown's Sugar House. He saw that a machine shop across the street was burning and noticed there were tiers of hogsheads piled up in front of the sugarhouse that would inevitably catch fire because of the intense heat and wind coming from the machine shop. It didn't take long before they were all burning and the windows in the sugarhouse seemed to melt and fall in, and in minutes it was burning like powder.

Mr. Sterling then moved on to Cotton Street and worked carrying water from wells to put on the flames. After a short stop at his house on Cumberland Avenue to change clothes, he went off looking for more ways he could be of help and never got home again until later the next day.

Sterling then went to work helping to move merchandise from various stores on Exchange Street to Post Office Square. The merchandise was all piled up in the streets and of course later burned.

Later, Mr. Sterling found himself in the city building when it actually caught fire. Prisoners there, who had been arrested that day, were released a short time later that same day. There was one prisoner who was overlooked inadvertently. According to Sterling, "About 10 o'clock the next forenoon, I was in the building, then mostly in ruins, when I heard a voice cry out. I crawled over the pile of bricks into the cell room, and found a man in cell 15. He had been overlooked when the cells were unlocked and had stayed where he was while the building burned over and around him. The cell was on the west side of the room and he got air, the high winds blowing into the room through an open window. The cell room, then as now, was partly finished in wood laid on brick and iron. The door to the patrolmen's room and then to the yard, had been burned out, and the woodwork in the east corridor of the cell room had been burned, but the man was not even scorched. Thanks to the open window, the high wind and the fact that he was on the west side instead of the east."

There was one other man, a policeman named Archibald Montgomery, who was at the top of the City Building looking for fire, who nearly did not make it out to safety. He was seen running down the stairs with his whiskers scorched and smoking.

You would think that a conflagration of such great proportion would by itself cause great damage. But some of the damage was purposely done to try to prevent even more destruction. Crews were sent out with barrels of powder and fuses in hopes of creating fire breaks. It was felt that by blowing up some strategically chosen buildings, a fire break would open, giving the flames nowhere else to go. This, it was hoped, would cause the flames to burn out. Desperate times call for desperate measures.

Mr. Sterling was chosen to be part of a team chosen for this task. He told the story in a newspaper article years after the fire. "I went with one of the parties sent out to blow up buildings. Deputy Marshal Alonzo Wentworth, Paul Field, and I started from the City Building at about six o'clock. We had two kegs of powder in the team and I was lying down holding a blanket over it, while sparks and flying brands rained down on us. We drove to Hugh Carney's house on Fore Street, near Plum. Then the fire was ripping along toward us. It had reached Cross Street. We put in one of the kegs of powder, set a fuse to it and touched it off. It did its business very completely. We also blew up the Blazier house on Plum Street."

Using explosives wasn't the only method used to try to stop the flames. Many small buildings were hauled down by using strong rope tied to a small anchor. It was then thrown over the house and a group of men would grab the line and pull as hard as they could. Ten or fifteen small buildings were removed this way.

One other incident involving Mr. Sterling is worth noting. In the early hours of the fire he learned that a Mr. Frank Floyd had been over-come by the heat. Mr. Sterling had been caught in a yard at the back of the burning sugarhouse. He managed to scale the wall and, dropping down onto Bank Street, found Mr. Floyd lying unconscious there, surrounded by a group of people helplessly standing around, doing nothing. It was discovered that Mr. Floyd was actually a fireman who had succumbed to the heat and smoke. Mr. Sterling, with some difficulty, was able to bring Mr. Floyd around and to his senses.

CHAPTER EIGHT
PANIC SETS IN

Fortunately, most people are spared the horror of having to experience the terror and fear of a great conflagration the size of the one that destroyed so much of Portland on July 4–5, 1866.

Once the alarming character of the blaze became apparent, along with the realization that Portland's fire department would not be able to handle the situation, panic began to spread throughout the city. The wind had risen and was blowing with the great violence of a gale. The streets were crowded with celebrating people and it was with the greatest of difficulty that they battled the fierce gusts of wind as it swept through the streets in a north-northeasterly direction.

The air was filled with sailing pieces of burning shingles that set fire to houses, leaving the owners with the tough task of trying to extinguish the flames. One resident told how his father-in-law was driving his buggy down from Munjoy Hill, accompanied by a lady passenger who was wearing a light summer dress. Several times her dress caught fire from the fiery shingles and cinders, and he had to drive with one hand and help put out the fire on her dress with his other hand. All in all it was a very perilous trip.

By the time realization of the calamity to come had set in, many residents seemed paralyzed with fear. The darkness had begun to replace the fading twilight and the glow of the flames and the roaring wind filled the sky with great flaming cinders. The air was filled with the sounds of wailing women, crying children, and cursing men.

A great number of people were trying to save their household goods while the merchants desperately tried to prevent their stock from being eaten by the flames. Free Street, above Hay's drug store, was filled for quite a distance with furniture and goods of every kind as the fire had spared that side of the street.

For those standing at the post office, it was hot as a fiery furnace as the air was filled with burning flakes of wood, and people's clothes would have great holes burned in them as they moved along the streets. Some folks, in their fright, got lost, and many were cut off by the rapid progress of the flames from reaching home by the usual routes. The great mass of people who lived downtown soon had no home to go to because the flames kept on their course until four or five o'clock in the morning of the fifth, when they finally exhausted themselves against the sandbank at the foot of Munjoy Hill.

CHAPTER NINE
THE POET'S SISTER

J ust up from what is now Monument Square and next door to the Preble House stands a three-story brick federal-style house, the oldest brick house on the Portland peninsula. Built over a two-year period from 1785 to 1786, it is the home that the Wadsworth and Longfellow families were brought up in. Built by Revolutionary War General Peleg Wadsworth, grandfather of the famous poet Henry Wadsworth Longfellow, it was here that Henry and his brothers and sisters were raised. By 1866, the poet was no longer a resident there, but he was a frequent visitor as his widowed sister, Anne Longfellow Pierce, was now the owner and primary resident.

The house had been struck by fire twice before. In 1814, when it stood only two stories high, an overheated fireplace sent sparks flying onto the roof, setting it ablaze and causing much damage not only to the roof but also the second floor and many of the furnishings. Stephen Longfellow, Henry and Anne's father, decided to add a third floor rather than just replacing the roof.

One other fire had touched the house when hot embers from a nearby house landed on the roof of an attached ell, which was saved by family members who kept the roof wet, preventing any serious damage. It did, however, leave Anne with a lifelong fear of the chance of the house burning down. The lack of an adequate citywide water system and the frequent use of fire in homes for cooking and heating always created a dangerous situation.

So it was on July 4, 1866, when Portland was struck by the greatest conflagration ever experienced in an urban area in the history of the United States.

At first, before things got out of hand, Anne was sure that the fire department would be able to handle the situation. But as the flames spread and conditions worsened, fear began to set in. As the flames swept closer and closer to what the family lovingly called the Old Original, Anne decided to send the young relatives visiting with her to the home of her brother Alexander who lived in a relatively safe area, an estate on Brighton Avenue called Highfield.

Brighton Avenue was not on the peninsula so it was not expected that the fire would be of any danger to that area.

It did not take long for the wind-driven flames to spread to buildings very close to the Longfellow house. Just a couple of short blocks east on Congress Street, City Hall had succumbed to the heat and winds and was now ablaze. Anne felt she could almost reach out and touch the fire. Diagonally across from City Hall stood a building that had once been called the Portland Academy, where a very young Henry Longfellow had been a student. It was one of the buildings chosen for demolition by dynamite to create a fire block. The whole scene created a very scary picture for the then fifty-five-year-old Anne.

Finally, on Thursday morning, July 6, at seven o'clock, with the situation finally beginning to settle down, Anne sat down and wrote a letter to her sister, Mary Greenleaf. She wrote, "Dearest Mary. We are all well, unharmed after a most terrific conflagration which swept through our city last night—beginning near the Sugar House soon after 4 P.M. and burning with tremendous furor till 4 this A.M. and still burning in the corner part of the city. The wind was very high. You have no idea what it is. There is not a single building standing from Fore Street to Court Street down through India to Washington Street. The P.O., Custom House—everything swept clean—everything—Elm House—Natural History—and the new City Hall building. The course of the fire was diagonally across the city from the Sugar House on York Street taking Gorham's Corner. Continue through to Spring—Cotton Street to Middle, through Federal, turning to Congress and Court—taking the City Hall, a fearful, fearful sight. The streets are full of homeless women and little children and furniture—. The children are safe at Highfield for the night. [Illegible] was very much frightened at the alarm so I hurried them all off in an early car for the guest of Highfield."

It was actually discovered later, in a note added to Anne's letter by Henry Wadsworth Dana, a relative who lived in the Craigie House in Cambridge, Mass., the poet's adult home, from 1917 to 1950. Dana did much research on all members of his family and discovered that Anne did not wait for the horse-drawn car to send her brother's children to Alexander Longfellow's Highfield home, but instead sent them off on foot. Mr. Dana wrote, adding a comment to Anne's letter, "The children, not wanting to wait for the horse car, walked all the way to Highfield. People seeing them passing by said, 'see the poor little children who have been burned out.' At Highfield, they were put in the room on the further end of the house so as not to see the burning Portland from the windows."

Anne's letter to her sister continued, "I have not been in bed or closed my eyes since the sunrise bells rung in the glorious 4th. The suffering and destitution will be fearful—so many burned out—only think—not a single store on Middle Street or Exchange, not a church below the First Parish or the Chestnut Street Methodist. Not a bank, not a lawyer's office or printing office left in the city or book store. The post office was on fire but not combustible. With love, Anne."

Anne was very lucky that the path of the wind-driven conflagration spared one of Portland's greatest historical treasures for future generations to enjoy. The flames came within two short blocks of the house. One small gust, one small change of direction, and the story could have had a different twist.

In 1901, with Anne's death, the Longfellow house was willed by her to the Maine Historical Society, specifically to be used as a house museum in memory of her family. Because of her foresight, and the will of the wind, people from around the world are still enjoying the Longfellow house.

CHAPTER TEN
THE GENERAL AND THE SUGARHOUSE

On August 8, 1862, John Marshall Brown, son of Sugar House owner John Bundy Brown, was commissioned first lieutenant and adjutant in the Twentieth Maine Regiment Volunteer Infantry. This was the regiment made famous on July 2, 1863, at Little Round Top during the battle of Gettysburg under the command of Joshua Chamberlain.

Throughout the Civil War, after displaying much bravery in many battles, John Marshall Brown rose rapidly through the ranks, finally receiving the breveted rank of colonel. On June 12, 1864, during the battle of Petersburg, he was seriously and, it was thought, mortally wounded. By September 23, 1864, he was discharged because of physical disability from his wounds. He was also breveted brigadier general for his gallant and meritorious service during the war.

Shortly after leaving the service, General Brown joined his father's firm, J.B. Brown and Sons, and also began to take on a number of civic duties. In 1866 he married Alida C. Carroll of Washington, D.C.

Brown was in Portland over the Fourth of July holiday, although his wife remained in Washington. She was not in favor of moving to Portland, so John spent much time commuting between the two cities. On July 6 he wrote a long, previously unpublished letter to Alida informing her of the situation in his hometown. He told her that three letters had arrived that very day and that they had come just in time, a time when he needed to hear some kindly words to "cheer and encourage me."

His letter continued, "I have been prevented from writing to you by sheer physical fatigue and weariness of body and soul and even now there are tears in my eyes and tears in my heart as I attempt to tell you of the appalling calamity that has fallen upon us here in Portland. Part of it you must have seen already in the newspapers."

John Marshall Brown had stopped in Boston just long enough on his trip to Portland to rest and try to recover from a "terrible headache." All in all, his trip took thirty-two hours and he arrived in Portland on July 3. On the afternoon of the holiday, Brown and a group of friends went to Glen Cove for a picnic. He continued in his letter to Alida that he expected to return early "for my part to take the evening for a long letter to you my best and dearest friend. How little we expected the frightful calamity which was to come. First as we were ordering the horses home-ward to return, a man came riding up most furiously and shouted out 'the Sugar House was burning.'" Brown continued to inform his wife of the story. "After the Sugar House was all gone we looked about us: no words can describe the woeful grandeur of the scene: as far as we could see to the northeast every building was on fire, the flames seemed to rise and the air was filled with flying cinders. It was evident that nothing could check the progress of the conflagration and the only course left was to save life and property."

At that point in his story, John Marshall Brown describes how he and his brother, who was with him, headed toward their grandmother's house, which was about a mile from the Sugar House.

"When we reached the Post Office we found it impossible to proceed any farther in that direction. When at last we reached grandmother's it was evident that her house must go. I took her in my arms, put her in a wagon, and carried her to Bramhall and then returned to save what we could: In less than a half hour afterward the house was destroyed. You cannot conceive the horror of the scene. The frame building seemed to burn up instantly. The noise of the flames was like a hurricane and wherever the hot blast swept everything went down before it."

Brown continued to do what he could through the night and, worn out early Thursday morning, was finally able to attend to some personal matters. His letter continued, "The general results of this conflagration are unparalleled in the history of the country. You have read in the newspapers but you can have no idea of it until you see the ruins. All of the city between the U. S. Hotel and the town on the hill is destroyed, absolutely wiped out. Every building on Middle and Exchange is gone. Every bank, printing office, 6 hotels and nearly a thousand dwelling-houses. The fire extended over a mile in length and a half-mile in breadth. Our house and that of the firm of J. B. Brown and sons are the heaviest losers. Father's individual loss being over a quarter of a million of dollars but we have not lost our courage or our faith. Father begins tomorrow to build some stores on the burned lots and as soon as we can clear away the debris we shall start another sugar house."

After the initial start of the fire and the realization the Sugar House could not be saved, John Marshall Brown devoted his time and energy to helping out however he could. He aided the firemen. "It seemed to me as if I had the strength of ten men. I worked in the hottest places, sometimes holding with the firemen the engine pump in the very face of the fire. Once I was nearly pushed off a high ladder and got badly burned. Once I was obliged to drop down holding the ladder with my hands. Of course I was drenched with water and thoroughly blackened with smoke. One of my eyes was burned also, but, thank heaven, I received no serious injuries. Since it was to no purpose, the magnificent building was entirely consumed with the contents and the labor of 25 years seems blotted out all-together. Father was very cool and collected although we felt very anxious about his ability to bear the blow."

He signed his letter with the nickname he used when he wrote to his wife, Giovanni.

CHAPTER ELEVEN
THE VIEW FROM THE HOUSE OF THE DEAD

One of the more fortunate Portland residents at the time of the great fire was Ruth Pierce Crocker, whose house was located in a section of the city that was not touched by the flames. On July 6 she sat down and told her sister in a letter, "We were providentially situated where the fire did not reach us and suffered only from anxiety and fear." She informed her sister that thousands had lost their places of employment and were out of work. "It would make your heart ache to see the sad, disconsolate faces and despairing looks which abound...It is said that there are eight thousand people without a house or a shelter. You can judge something of the distress and confusion that abounds. The sidewalks are literally covered with furniture."

William Willis wrote in his journal on Sunday, July 8, that is was the hottest day of the season, with the temperature climbing to ninety-three degrees. "At 5 a shower came and the mercury fell to 74; a brief and light shower with three or four claps of thunder. The lightning struck the State Street church spire and set it on fire but it was soon extinguished. Rev. Calvin Stebbins preached but instead of a sermon he gave some appropriate remarks relating to our recent calamity—Instances are constantly coming to ones knowledge of distressing cases of losses by the fire by which deserving women have been deprived of all their means and even their clothing."

The day before, on Saturday, the seventh, the mayor wisely ordered all barrooms and saloons that had not been destroyed to remain closed.

And all the fireworks that were provided for the great celebration of the Fourth were carted to Back Cove and unceremoniously heaved into the water. The population had had more than their share in recent days.

John Neal in his *Account of the Great Conflagration in Portland* describes a number of interesting incidents that are worth repeating. Some of them are solemn and some laughable, as may be expected in a disaster as great as that in Portland.

One story was told by Charles P. Illsley, describing what he saw at the Eastern Cemetery during the height of the fire.

"About three o'clock on the morning of the 5th of July, we made our way to Commercial Street, passing through Fore Street, which, from Center nearly to India Street, on its upper side, was one unbroken mass of flames looking with it sinuosities like a monstrous, writhing, fiery serpent. From Commercial we proceeded to Mountfort Street, until we reached the eastern boundary of the burial ground. At this period we had the whole fearful spectacle before us. The wind was blowing a perfect gale, whirling clouds of dust into the air.

"We stood at the entrance of the graveyard. Houseless men, women, and children were seated in scattered groups about the place, looking as if the tenants of the tombs and graves had come forth to witness the appalling scene. Overhead, lurid clouds of smoke rolled wildly away toward the north, whence descended an incessant shower of fiery rain. The flames had not reached India, and the lower part of Congress Streets, but for a mile or more before, and on each side of us, was one vast raging sea of fire where billows of flames were tossed tumultuously to and fro, surging and roaring as we have seen and heard the Atlantic [ocean] from the Cape during a fierce tempest. Occasionally, a gigantic billow would dash against some tall building, causing the flaming surf and the sparkling spray to leap high into the heavens. On and on swept the fire demons, lapping up in an instant, as it were, and destroying the homes of men.

"Amid the crackling of burning timber, the roaring of the fiery billows, and the rush of the gale, came the crash of falling buildings, the muffled explosions of houses and stores razed to the ground, the shriek of the steam fire engines, and the cries of the excited multitude…It was a scene that would never pass from memory."

The *Portland Daily Advertiser* wrote the story of the near-death experience of claim agent Z.K. Harmon, who was trapped in his office in the U. S. Post Office and Custom House building with no apparent way of escape on the night of the Fourth of July. Exit to Exchange Street was impossible because flames were shooting out from the Eck Block and the heat was forcing large rocks off the walls of the building like someone with a sledgehammer was smashing them to the ground. The sidewalks and the street were so hot that they were literally glowing red. According to the article, "a perfect sea of flame rolled up from the lower part of Exchange Street on the front, while on Lime Street the intense heat from the Sturdivant House and the new printing house of the Advertiser, just finishing both wooden buildings, perfectly enveloping the U. S. building in sheets of flame."

The only hope for Mr. Harmon was in the endurance of the building he was trapped in.

"On Thursday morning, an Irish boy was seen about the 'dump' with something he supposed to be lead. The nugget was examined and proved to be silver. It could not have weighed less than three pounds. The boy said he found it in the cellar of St. Stephen's Church, where, by the way, Mrs. John M. Wood had lodged her best furniture, plate, and jewels for safety in the hurry and confusion of breaking up, which were destroyed together with the church itself, in two or three hours."

Flocks of doves, as they were driven from the church towers and other places, would fly off beyond the fire into the darkness and then return toward the light, and flying high above the hurricane of fire cinders, would drop into the abyss below.

An Irish woman was seen carrying off a large pig from the midst of the flames, leaving her baby to take care of itself, told people her 'darlint' was safe. Another was seen chasing a pig at full speed with her clothes flying loose and hair streaming, like a meteor down Center Street. The pig made a dash at a heap of furniture, followed by the woman with loud outcries. A few moments later, while she was poking around after him, he reappeared with a washstand upon his back, through the legs of which he had thrust himself, and not being able to get rid of it, he was now seen hurrying away, like a miniature elephant, with a tower on his back, at full speed, followed by his poor mistress in a transport of terror."

Neal continues with his Irish tale during the fire. "An Irishman was hard at work on Center Street, unmindful of a great blaze coming toward him like a tornado. A friend called 'Look at the fire Pat!' 'Faith and bejebers, it's all on fire' says Pat and went on with his work."

When the morning of the fifth dawned, it presented a scene of great confusion. Outside the burnt sections of the city and in the outskirts; the passageways, backyards, and doorsteps; the wharves and alleys were heaped with household goods and furniture, while here and there groups of pale, frightened survivors and whole families exhausted and asleep were lying wherever they could find a space that would offer them some comfort.

John Neal continued his report: "The following, one of a hundred similar scenes, occurred near the dump, a large empty space on the Cove: A little family were gathered together near a spot where, only a few hours before, stood their happy home; the father, seated on a little heap of household stuff, which he had saved from the flames; and as he sat there with eyes fixed upon the ground, and twisting a stick between his fingers, his two half naked children at his knees and wife standing before him with large silent tears rolling down her cheeks, trying to comfort him, it was really too piteous for description, and the spectator turned away speechless and left them to look for consolation elsewhere."

Ironically, some of the houses that were destroyed were houses that had escaped unscathed during the 1775 British bombardment of Portland, then called Falmouth Neck. The buildings destroyed then amounted to more than three-quarters of the town.

Despite the confusion, terror, and danger of the conflagration, there were many cases of drunkenness. Maine was a prohibition state but many people had barrels of prohibited liquor, which they tried to save by rolling their barrels out onto the street where they thought they would be safe from the flames, only to see them carried off by strangers or destroyed by the flames.

John Neal writes of one case where an aged citizen was seen steaming up Exchange Street with a two-gallon tin measure in his hand, closely followed by a wall of flames. "On reaching the grocery store on the corner of Exchange and Federal Streets, he tumbled into a large box. Very soon however, an unmanageable horse being led on the sidewalk contrived to kick the box over and tumbled the old gentleman out upon the pavement. He was then helped off by a fireman, just when he was in danger of being roasted alive, for the flames were now roaring around that very corner. He was next found lying under the suction hose of one of the engines, near the curb stone by the city building. Being helped out of this difficulty, he disappeared for a time; but it suddenly having occurred to a policeman that there were ten kegs of powder in the police office, and fearing the terrible consequences of an explosion, he hurried off to the building which was then all on fire. As he entered the passage-way he stumbled over some-thing, which upon being dragged to the light, proved to be the same old fellow. He was then taken below Cumberland Street and left there, while the policeman and others removed the powder."

CHAPTER TWELVE
THE MAYOR SPEAKS

n his annual report for the fiscal year 1866-67 to the Portland Board of Aldermen, Mayor Augustus E. Stevens clarified the great conflagration picture. He told the board members, "Eight months ago, while yet in the enjoyment of the festivities in honor of our national anniversary, we were suddenly called by the usual alarm to extinguish a fire in the southerly part of the city, which although at first exciting no serious apprehension, it soon became evident would tax the energies of our firemen to the utmost to subdue….The efforts of our fire department, which we had labored under the delusion of being invincible, and of those companies from other cities and towns who so nobly responded to our cry for help, were of no avail; the conflagration swept on, increasing in extent and destructiveness consuming everything in its course, until it reached the northern limits of the city, and only there stopped for want of material to feed upon."

There have been various estimates of the loss, most of them based on the physical destruction of property, of up to $12 million in 1866 dollars ($120 million today). What should be added to the value is the great loss sustained by the interruption to business, which is difficult to determine.

The city itself lost about half a million dollars including City Hall, the old State House, four schoolhouses, and three engine houses. Adding greatly to the large loss was the increase in city debt due to the cost of dealing with the fire and its aftermath. This all came at a time when taxes were already too high.

Particularly problematical were the loss of the schoolhouses. Taken away from students were: the two-story brick building on Franklin Street, occupied by primary school number 3; two-story building on Congress Street occupied by the grammar school for girls and primary school number 9; the two-story brick building on Congress Street near the Eastern Cemetery, occupied by the grammar school for boys; and the one-story brick building in the rear occupied by primary school number 13. There were in all about one thousand students affected. To offset this situation somewhat, the city council approved the school committee's application to build two temporary schoolhouses on Congress Street, one near the corner of Market Street and the other near Locust Street. Cost of construction was just over four thousand dollars.

July 31, an order was passed by the city council for building a large and substantial permanent schoolhouse on Congress Street near the Eastern Cemetery, to be named North School. The building still stands and is now used for senior citizen living quarters.

Before the fire, Portland policemen were not overly taxed because the city was "unusually quiet and free from disorderly persons." However, the situation changed dramatically because of the great fire. The mayor's report to the aldermen continued, "The tidings of our disaster brought in among us from the larger cities, a multitude of rough and desperate characters who considered the confusion which existed favorable for their operations. The fear and anxiety of our people was for a time painful. Many armed themselves and kept nightly watch to protect their property."

For a time, the situation looked grim and dangerous, but it did not take long for Portland residents to react. The first step was to hire more bodies to patrol the city, and a large force of special police was put in place. The government sent two companies, one of marines and one of regulars, to help control those who were looking to enrich themselves illegally. Because of all this extra help, few serious crimes were committed and it did not take long before order and quiet were soon restored and the bad guys left Portland as quietly as they had come.

One of the consequences of the great fire was the implementation of a better way of notifying the fire department when a fire broke out. In November of 1866 the city contracted for installing a fire alarm telegraph at a cost of $5,300 that would "greatly facilitate the giving of alarms and indicating the location of fires."

In another municipal report, the chief engineer of the fire department, Spencer Rogers, listed his recommendations to alleviate what was perhaps one of the major faults of Portland and a great contributor to the difficulty of fighting the 1866 fire: the lack of a sufficient supply of water. Most of the city's water supply came from wells and cisterns, and a must for each home were leather water fire buckets.

After the fire, little money was spent to increase the water supply until the lack of sufficient water led to the formation in 1867 of the Portland Water Company, whose mission was to bring water from nearby Sebago Lake to the city. By July 4, 1870, water finally began flowing into the city.

Engineer Rogers in the meantime, recommended that a few necessary steps be taken to rectify the situation. He called for "a reservoir to be built on the corner of Pine and Carlton Streets, and a reservoir on the corner of Brackett and Pine Streets be enlarged." He also recommended that other cisterns and reservoirs be enlarged. He wrote,

> "The season was very dry and the buildings, heated by the sun, were ready to kindle from a spark of fire. The first engine that arrived, for some cause, would not take water. The second and third that arrived lost much valuable time in consequence of burning hose. Before the fourth was ready to work, a second fire was reported on Union Street, and she was sent to take care of that.
>
> "It soon became evident to me that our fire department was inadequate to stop the fire and appeals for help were telegraphed to Lewiston, Gardner, Bath, Biddeford, Hallowell, and Augusta, and a special train was sent to Saco. Before this relief could reach us, the fire was past control.
>
> "As is generally believed that the July fire was caused by fire crackers, and as their use is always attended with risk of conflagration I would recommend the passage of an ordinance making it penal to keep or sell firecrackers."

Firecrackers were ultimately banned in the state of Maine for many years until 2012, when they were made legal by the state legislature, with the condition that individual cities and towns could ban them in their locations. Portland did vote to keep them illegal.

After July of 1866, Portland did purchase some new equipment. A new steam fire engine, made in Portland by the Portland Company, was bought for $4,500 to take the place of the destroyed engine number 5, and a new hook-and-ladder truck was purchased for $750. Also 3,250 feet of leather and 400 feet of rubber hose were purchased.

CHAPTER THIRTEEN
AFTERMATH

When the great Portland conflagration finally subsided, the city's citizens began to consider the consequences other than their own. Their way of everyday living would no longer be recognizable to them; the stores they were used to doing business with were now just a pile of ashes in many cases, their daily routines would no longer be the same. Many residents now had no jobs or a place to sleep or changes of clothing. They had nothing. Many things that directly affected them were now changed, and they had to seriously consider their future hopes and prospects.

John Neal wrote, "Let us remember first how much we have to be thankful for, and how much more destructive the visitation must have been had it happened in mid-winter, or at dead of night, or both these conditions had coincided. Owing to the timely notice we had, to the favorable season and the pleasant weather, only two lives were lost and they might have been lost by a common fire in the house the parties occupied, for both were helpless from intoxication."

Actually, there is a possibility that three people died as a result of the fire. In his book *Burial Records 1717–1962 of the Eastern Cemetery*, historian William B. Jordan lists three deaths: Susan Bluefield, whose body was entirely consumed in the house in which she lived on Fore Street. Her death was not known until February 1891, when it was revealed in an affidavit signed by two people, Ephraim Webster and his wife, Elizabeth. It is not known why they waited so long before they revealed the information. The other victims were Elizabeth Chickering and her daughter Zabrina.

Another reason Portland citizens had to be thankful was the dry, pleasant weather that continued for such a long spell after the fire. This allowed ample time for shelter to be provided to those who lost their residences.

John Neal continued, "We have had the most favorable weather for all kinds of labor, for rebuilding to advantage and for living in tents; and though it has been warmer than was ever known here for so long a time, and the heat of the ruins and the dust—without smoke—have been unsupportable, with the thermometer up to ninety-six, ninety-eight, and one hundred and three, the labor of cleaning up, and preparing for speedy renovation has never been suspended for a single hour, even where the very pavements were calcined, the street railways warped into all sorts of contortions, and deep cellars were glowing like so many furnaces, with hard and soft coal, and with the few half smothered fragments of timbers that were not charred through and through, or reduced to ashes; and the plentiful rains we have since had—after the poor outcasts were sheltered, having mostly fallen at night."

News of Portland's misfortune was covered by newspapers all across the country, and almost immediately help in many forms began to arrive in the city. As John Neal wrote, "It has touched the hearts and awakened the sympathy, and secured the help of thousands and tens of thousands throughout our whole country and over the sea; the contributions in cash, having already amounted to over $500,000, and in clothing, food, building material and labor, to at least $100,000 more."

Most people thought that the insurance companies would be so deeply affected by all the claims that would be filed, that the companies would more than likely have to fail and that claims would be well over $15 million or $20 million ($100 million to $200 million in today's dollars). Within a few days, however, after actual claims were paid, only two of the many insurance companies had difficulty, both because their home offices were totally destroyed. By August, the *Portland Advertiser* reported that $3,159,450 (over $30 million today) had already been paid without "quibble or delay."

The day after the fire subsided, cleanup began. John Bundy Brown, the largest loser financially, declared that the "real estate of Portland was worth more the day after, than the day before the fire." Businessmen discovered that it cost more to lease store lots on Exchange Street than it did before the fire, and those purchasing house lots found that they were forced to pay more than double the average price they would have paid on the third of July. Many times the burned wreckage of the destroyed buildings was still on the lots, causing the added expense of removal of the old before anything new could be built.

John Neal noted in his report, published in August 1866, "We have underway, and nearly completed for occupation, about 300 houses and stores, and everywhere, within the business parts of town and along the outskirts, the cellars are emptied of the bricks and rubbish, the streets cleared, the walls run up, and whole blocks of stores on their way, to be larger and handsomer than ever, though not always as high, by one story, as they were before."

Portlanders, it seems, were not letting the grass grow under their feet.

Neal continued, "Let us see what may be reasonably expected hereafter. That great improvements will be made is clear. New streets are to be opened, others are to be widened and straightened, and we are to have what we always wanted, a public square in the very heart of the city, which of course, will add greatly to the value of the property in the neighborhood, and to the comfort and health of our people."

What John Neal was referring to was the creation of Lincoln Park, which lies diagonally across the street from City Hall, placed there to act as a fire break in the event Portland ever suffered another great fire. The park is bounded by Congress, Franklin, Federal, and Pearl Streets. It was purchased by a committee appointed by the city council on July 9, for $83,000.

Another contract was approved to enclose the lot with a substantial iron fence. The park stands as an example of how quickly the city government can act if it wants to.

Neal continued,

"Our great commercial thoroughfare is untouched. Our wholesale grocers, flour dealers, and commission dealers have escaped altogether, and even our wholesale dry goods dealers, shoe and leather dealers, jobbers, and manufacturers, and machinists have had but a light scorching. Our retailers are all at work once more. Our banks are all re-established. All our insurance offices, and printing offices, and newspaper establishments are in full blast—and all our doctors and lawyers. We had, and still have, one of the best harbors in the world; with facilities for shipping and manufacturing almost unequalled....Our city had become a proverb in all parts of the earth.

"And what is it now? Changed in nothing but in the loss of buildings, soon to be replaced, more beautiful and more convenient than ever. That thousands of the poor have been living in tents, upon public charity for a while, though the number of rations has been reduced from 7,200 to about 500 per day, and all who are willing to work…may have constant employment and our worst neighborhoods have been purged by fire; that many of our worthiest fellow citizens, our mechanics and laborers, our milliners and dress makers, and our work women of all kinds, have been impoverished, just when most of them had begun to feel comfortable and secure, must be acknowledged. They will not be allowed to suffer, and for the next two or three years we shall be among the busiest; and if we are wise, among the happiest and most thankful communities to be found."

John Neal's autobiography, detailing the period of reconstruction from 1866 to 1868, captures the activities and feelings of the times.

"Dec. 8, 1866—our fine weather still continues, the most favorable for building. We have rain almost every night, beginning after the day's work is over, and clearing off before the laborers begin anew in the morning; and then we have it almost always clear and pleasant. Portland is going up, not as on the last Fourth of July, in a chariot of fire, but with the calm, stately movement, and occasional magnificence, that we should look for in a material resurrection.

"Dec. 26th, 1866—our fine weather still continues. The earth is bare of snow, and today we are getting our roofs on by the score.

"Jan. 27th, 1867—within the last month…we have had two of the toughest and heaviest snow storms I ever saw and are now up to the waist in another…

"And yet, our people are swarming to their work, early and late, through the deep snow; block after block, and street after street."

CHAPTER FOURTEEN
RECONSTRUCTION

Portlanders lost no time beginning the tough job of cleaning up after the flames died down. They began sifting through the ashes of their homes and businesses, first to see if there was anything they could save, which was very little, but more importantly to begin the tough job of clearing away the rubble to allow construction of new homes, stores, and offices so that their lives and incomes could resume normalcy.

There was more than just the physical building to do. There was much of Mother Nature to replace. John Neal wrote, "Our trees!—Our beautiful trees; the boast of our city and the admiration of strangers, are not wholly destroyed, even in the burned district. Thousands still 'do live' and the charred trunks are sprouting afresh, with living emerald, and the branches are feathering out like plants in a tropical region after the terrible forcing they have had to undergo 'all greenly fresh and wildly free.' Nevertheless, we have lost where they were most crowded and where a large portion of them could be spared, no less than 625.

"Much labor and expense and the patient waiting of three score years will be required to reproduce them in all their glorious exuberance of foliage and ponderance weight of limb overreaching some of our widest thoroughfares."

The weather for the reconstruction activities continued to remain favorable, and by the end of August 1866, there had been much progress. More than 300 buildings were in advanced stages of completion.

Insurance money had been forthcoming relatively quickly, and cash contributions through August had grown to well over $600,000, coming from all directions. Newspaper stories about the great fire had appeared all over the country, and the money began to flow into Portland almost immediately from places like New York, Boston, Philadelphia, Cleveland, St. Louis, and nearly all of New England. Donations even arrived from across the Canadian border from St. John, New Brunswick, and Montreal.

John Neal estimated that the reconstruction would be completed within two years.

There were even local activities going on to help those Portland residents in need. One example was Friday evening, July 20. An amateur theatrical group put on a performance of *Buckstone's Comedy of Married Life*, followed by the laughable farce, *Who Stole the Pocketbook?* The performance was held at Granite Hall with tickets selling for fifty cents each.

There were also restrictive building measures issued by the city in an attempt to prevent any further fire disasters in the future. On July 21, 1866, an ordinance was issued by the mayor, Augustus E. Stevens, and Charles M. Rice, president of the board of aldermen, governing the construction of wooden buildings. It read, "Concerning the erection of wooden buildings. Be it enacted by the Mayor, Aldermen, and Common Council of the City of Portland, in City Council assembled as following:

> "Section 1, No Building or buildings, the exterior walls of which shall be in part or wholly of wood, exceeding ten feet in height, shall hereafter be erected in this city without permission in each case from the Mayor or Aldermen.
>
> "Section 2, No building or buildings, the exterior walls of which shall be in part or wholly of wood shall be permitted or allowed to be erected in that part of the city, including within the following limits, viz: Commencing on Congress Street at the head of Center Street, thence through said Congress Street to Pearl Street to Middle Street, thence through Middle to Franklin Street, thence through Franklin to the center of Commercial Street, thence through Commercial Street to Center Street. Thence through Center Street to Congress Street, the place of beginning including both sides of the above named streets, excepting the southern side of Commercial Street.

"Section 3, It shall be the duty of the City Marshall to cause to be removed at once, as nuisance, all buildings erected in violation of this ordinance."

The streets themselves were not neglected; work began to widen and lengthen many streets in the burned-out districts. For example, there was a pronounced curve on Middle Street which was straightened; Exchange and Temple Streets were widened; and Pearl, Anderson, and Franklin Streets were all widened.

City Hall was gutted by the flames and a new one began to rise from the shell of the destroyed building. And the government constructed a new post office and customs house. Many churchgoers saw new places of worship spring up to replace sanctuaries that that had gone up in flames.

New brick blocks arose throughout the business district like those at Pearl and Middle Streets and Temple Street. Many more came in the following months.

In 1867, the Portland Water Company was organized to bring water from Sebago Lake to Portland via pipeline. It was much needed, as Portland's water supply at the time of the great conflagration was considered primitive. The only sources of the precious liquid came from reservoirs, cisterns, wells, springs, and the ocean. The pipeline was finally finished on July 4, 1870, bringing the city into a more modern and safer time.

By November of 1866, the *New Hampshire Sentinel* in Keene, N.H., reported, "About a thousand buildings are in course of erection in the burnt district of Portland, or are under contract. One master mason has 450 men in his employ, and the payroll of all hands in the burnt district amounts to $750,000 per week. The streets have been widened and straightened, squares laid out and the section generally much improved."

Many of Portland's hotels had burned to the ground, causing much inconvenience to the city's many visitors. Some of the hotels destroyed were the American House, Commercial House, Elm House, International House, Kingsbury's Hotel, Freeman House, and Fulton House. They were gradually replaced as new hotels opened and undamaged hotels were enlarged and remodeled. One of the largest new hotels was built by John Bundy Brown, the largest loser financially. He built the Falmouth Hotel on Middle Street, one of the largest and most luxurious hotels in New

England. It was torn down in the 1960s.

Neal continued the summary of his reconstruction progress report:

> "May 23rd, 1867—Portland is going up, and all the buildings that were got underway soon after the fire, and up to mid-winter, have been finished, with improvements a hundred years in advance of what they were before the fire; and most of them are already occupied, and all of the rest will be within a month; while others are going up, stores and mansions and large public buildings in every part of the town.
>
> "Sept. 22nd, 1867—there is probably more 'building' now underway that makes little show than there has been at any time since the fire. At first, every store, every shed or shanty, could be seen from every part of the city as it went up; but now that whole streets have been rebuilt, and high buildings are interposed by the acre, we have to turn off into cross-streets and by-ways to see what is going on.
>
> "All the stores and houses are occupied as fast as they are finished, and sometimes barely inhabitable; though the number is much greater than before the fire in all our leading thoroughfares and business quarters; and all this, in less than 14 months since a third of the city was laid to ashes.
>
> "Jan. 1st, 1868—Another year! Portland is now rebuilt and greatly enlarged and beautified."

In a 100th-anniversary celebratory article that appeared in the *Portland Press Herald*, the paper noted regarding the rebuilding of the city, "Many felt that it had advanced at least fifty years, because of the opportunity for rebuilding on a larger scale and in a better style. Having met the challenge off the Great Fire, the city faced the future with the confidence of old John Neal, who asked in 1874, '… What is there to stay our progress hereafter …?'"

APPENDIX A
LIST OF STREETS, BUILDINGS, AND BUSINESSES BURNED

Over the passage of time, it becomes evident that one of the most important documents still available to us is *John Neal's Account of the Great Conflagration in Portland, July 4th & 5th, 1866.* It is perhaps the most complete work on the fire and, as it turns out, the most valuable. It was published a short time after the fire, when the event was still locked in the minds of those who lived through it and their experiences still fresh. As the years passed, the incidents that occurred began to dim in memory, and facts and incidents became clouded to the point where victim's stories were, perhaps, not as true as they once were.

One-third of all the gas meters that were in use were destroyed. And the amount of gas wasted because of the broken pipes and other sources amounted to thousands of dollars.

Neal developed his list of the destruction from many sources, including the *Boston Journal* of July 7, 1866. The following list is taken from Neal's account and really emphasizes the tremendous amount of destruction that was caused by one firecracker. Without the list, it is difficult for one to grasp the tremendous amount of destruction.

On Commercial Street, where the heaviest houses are established, with a few exceptions, every building on the north side is gone, from the coal office of W. H. Evans to Cotton Street.

On York Street—Every building on the south side to Danforth Street; on the north, three buildings next above Maple Street, and all below Maple and Danforth.

On Maple Street—All the buildings between York and Danforth, except one upon the corner of Maple and Danforth.

Danforth Street—All the buildings on the south side, from Maple to Fore Streets, and all on the north side from the Gore house.

On Center Street—Brick building on the western corner, and all the buildings on the eastern side, nearly up to Spring Street.

On Cotton Street—Three buildings on the west side, near Fore Street, and six or eight on the other side.

On Plum Street—Every building on both sides, and among them the house of Dr. Carruthers, and the Portland Athenaeum.

On Myrtle Street—From Congress to Cumberland, nothing on the westerly side is gone but the City Hall; on the east, all destroyed, except one dwelling house on the corner of Cumberland.

On Exchange Street—A mass of ruins on both sides. Corey's large furniture establishment, all the book stores, jewelers' shops, insurance offices, banks and everything, save the Custom House, from Fore Street to Congress Street.

On Lime and Milk Streets—Everything swept away, with Milk Street and Warren Market, through to Congress Street.

On Temple Street—Everything in ashes from Middle to Congress Street, on east side, and to Federal on the west.

On Free and Middle Streets—Free Street block, all gone, except Mr. Tolford's large store; and every building on Middle Street from Free Street to India, except the store of D. F. Emery & Sons. Here were the principal dry goods establishments.

On Federal Street—Shop of Marr Brothers, and Dr. Mason's apothecary shop were saved; on the south side, every building from Chase & Co.'s hardware store, inclusive, to India Street gone, and on the north, every building from the Elm House to India Street.

On Congress Street—From Temple to India on the north side, up to, and including the Catholic School, above Washington Street, and on the south side, everything.

On Cumberland Street—On the south side, all the buildings from Myrtle to Washington Street, and thence up Munjoy, are gone; and on the north side, all the buildings from the Radford frame house, corner of Pearl.

On Oxford Street—Upper part all gone on both sides.

On Washington Street—Large number of houses destroyed—number cannot be correctly ascertained.

On Fore Street—With the exception of three stores belonging to the estate of John Fox, every building on the north side from Center Street is destroyed; on the south side, from Cross to India, not a building suffered.

On Cross Street—Both sides, from Fore to Middle Street, completely destroyed.

Union Street—All gone; all the shoe and leather stores, Winslow's machine shop, Grant's coffee and spice factory, and every building on both sides.

Other Streets—On Silver, Willow, Vine, Deer, Chatham, Franklin and Hampshire Streets, every building was destroyed, - and with them Sebastopol, the Gomorrah of Portland.

In addition to those before mentioned are the following streets and courts, either wholly or partially destroyed:

Bradley's Lane—wholly.

Stephenson's Court—wholly.

Bank Street—wholly.

Maple Street—partially.

Fox Court—wholly.

Ashland Avenue—wholly.

Garden Street—wholly.

Church Street—wholly.

Harrison Place—wholly.

Fremont Place—wholly.

Sumner Street—everything to India and greater part of the buildings beyond.

Chapel Street —wholly above Cumberland.

Quincy Street —wholly.

Wilmot Street —From Congress to Cumberland, wholly; several buildings below Cumberland.

Locust Street—wholly.

Mayo Street —partially.

Smith Street —wholly, from Congress to Oxford.

Boyd Street —partially.

Poplar Street—partially.

Larch Street—wholly.

Anderson Street— partially.

York Place—wholly.

Ingraham's Court—wholly.

Dyer Street —partially.

North Street—five buildings.

India Court—wholly.

Hancock Court—wholly.

Montgomery Street—wholly.

Abyssinian Court—wholly.

APPENDIX B
LARGE BLOCKS AND
PUBLIC BUILDINGS DESTROYED

Hall of Portland Society of Natural History, Congress Street, with all the furniture and collections, for the second time. This noble institution, founded and supported by private subscriptions, had just begun to carry out another of its great purposes, by a course of free lectures. It organized in 1835—was transferred to the Custom House building, where it lost everything by the fire of 1854. Again it was built up, and had gathered to itself, through the liberality of the State, in granting a half township, and by the help of individual contributions, property worth at least $25,000 or $30,000. It has now lost everything but a few books, and a portrait of Humboldt, from Mr. H.W. Longfellow, and must begin anew for the third time, undismayed and hopeful.

Portland Athenaeum—Founded in 1826; opened Jan. 1, 1827; established on the remains of the old Library Association, which was destroyed with the town in 1775—revived in 1784, and continued to this time with encouraging success; its new and very handsome building on Plum Street, erected in 1861, at a cost of $20,000, utterly destroyed, together with library off eleven thousand volumes. Library insured for $4000; building, in Portland Mutual, for $2000.

Young Men's Christian Association—Instituted 1843, lost everything; 1000 volumes in library.

Mercantile Library Association—Established in 1851. Lost everything with a library containing over 3,000 volumes. They have just received a donation of 500 volumes from the New York Mercantile Library Association; and 200 volumes from the Boston Mercantile Library Association.

Swedenborgian Church, Congress Street—Built in 1847.

Third Parish Church, Congress Street—Built in 1809. Occupied by two societies before the present.

Bethel, or Seamen's Church, Fore Street—First organized 1827. Church built in 1847.

First Baptist Church, Federal Street—Built in 1803; rebuilt and enlarged in 1811.

Church of the Immaculate Conception, Cumberland Street—Built in 1846. Cost, about $26,000. Value of all the buildings connected with it, over $140,000. To be rebuilt and ready for occupation in November next.

St. Stephen's Episcopal Church, Pearl Street—First built in 1802; rebuilt and greatly enlarged in 1839.

Second Parish, Congregational Church, Middle Street—Built in 1788. Enlarged for Dr. Payson, about 1826.

First Universalist Church, Pearl Street—Built in 1821. Cost $6,000.

Casco Bank Building, Middle Street—Erected in 1850. Cost $14,000.

Cumberland Bank—Incorporated in 1812 as the Maine Bank, and so continues for ten years. All our banks suffered severely in the great commercial convulsion and paralysis of 1837 and 1838: in Portland they lost half their capital.

Ocean Insurance Company's blocks of three stores, Exchange and Milk Streets—built in 1860.

City Hall, Congress Street—A magnificent pile, with front of Albert stone, and wings and rear of brick and Albert stone. Here were all the town offices, county offices, court-rooms and record offices, corporation rooms, and one of the largest and handsomest public halls in the country. Built in 1862–3. Cost, $264,000. James H. Rand, architect.

Custom House and Post Office—Begun for Exchange and stores, in 1839. Cost $100,000. Bought by the General Government for Custom House, Post Office, and U.S. Courts and offices fire-proof, in 1855. An appropriation of $100,000 has just been made by Congress for repairing, but it will have to be taken down and wholly rebuilt.

Sugar House—Portland Sugar Company—Building begun in 1845.

Estimated value of sugar house building before fire	$118,410.00
Estimated salvage	$11,500.00
Amount of loss	$106,910.00
Value of machinery destroyed	$161,128.70
Stock in sugar house destroyed	$254,492.75
Total loss	$522,532.00
Total amount of insurance	$275,000.00
Actual net loss to company	$247,432.45

The fire is still burning here, (August 22) burning, though charred to a coal, is carted away.

Wood's Marble Hotel, Middle Street—built in lathed and plastered. Cost $140,000.

Large Block, built by Mr. J. M. Wood, corner of Middle and Silver Streets. Owed by J. E. Donnell. Occupied for dry goods and whole-sale shoe and leather business. Masonic Hall in upper story handsomely finished and furnished—nothing saved but Lodge jewels, records and charters.

Block on opposite corner, built in 1850 by J.C. Proctor. Cost of both blocks, $60,000.

Granite Block, on Middle Street—built in 1830 by Martin Gore, William Swan and others. Withstood both of the great Temple Street fires.

Large Block on Middle Street, opposite Post Office, known as Advertiser Building. Built in 1856 by John M. Wood at a cost of $14,000. Free Street Block—built in 1853–54 by F. O. Libby and others. Cost $60,000. Mussey's Block, Middle Street—erected in 1856. Cost about $80,000. Wholly burned down three times and partially once. On the same spot where Mr. Mussey lived when a boy; being rebuilt each time. The first bricks on Middle Street, after the fire, were laid here August 1.

Hanson's block, Middle Street—Built in 1857. Cost $15,000.

Barbour Block, Middle Street—Built by H.N. Jose in 1850. Cost $20,000.

Fox Block, on Exchange Street—built in 1853–54. Cost $75,000.

Jose Block, on Exchange Street—built in 1856. Cost $22,000. The Odd Fellows' hall was in this building. Three Lodges and two Encampments held their meetings there. Nothing saved but charters and records. Loss, $3,500; insured for $1,500.

Thomas Block, Exchange Street—Built in 1855. Cost $25,000.

Jones's Row, Exchange Street—Built in 1800; rebuilt and greatly enlarged in 1838 and 1844.

SOURCES

BOOKS

Burial Records 1717–1962 of the Eastern Cemetery, compiled by William B. Jordan Jr., Heritage Books, 1987

Maine's Visible Black History, H.H. Price & Gerald E. Talbot, Tilbury House, 2008

A Man from Maine, Edward Bok, 1923

A Short History of Portland, Allan M. Levinsky, Commonwealth Editions, 2008

A Time of Men, J. Donald MacWilliams, Monmouth Press, 1967

PUBLICATIONS

Account of the Great Conflagration in Portland, July 4th & 5th, 1866, John Neal, Starbird & Twitchell, 1866

The Portland Fire of 1866, Peter L. Hall, 2007

NEWSPAPERS

The Daily Constitution Union, Washington, D.C., July 1866

Daily Memphis Avalanche, Memphis, Tenn., November 1866

Macon Daily Telegraph, Macon, Ga., July 1866

Portland Advertiser, Portland, Maine, June 1866

Portland Daily Press, Portland, Maine, June 1866, July 1866, August 1866

Portland Eastern Argus, Portland, Maine, August 1866

Portland Evening Express, Portland, Maine, Earle G. Shettleworth Jr., 1966 anniversary edition

Portland Evening Star, Portland, Maine, July 1866

Portland Sunday Telegram, Portland, Maine, October 1929

New Hampshire Sentinel, Keene, N.H., November 1866

New York Times, July 1866, October 1922

The Sun, Baltimore, Md., July 1866, August 1866

REPORTS

City of Portland Annual Report, March 1867

Dedication of Lincoln Park, City of Portland, February 1909

Portland Municipal Reports, 1866, 1867

MAGAZINES

American Architect, September 1912

LETTERS

John Marshall Brown, to wife, July 6, 1866, (courtesy Maine Historical Society)

Ruth C. Crocker, July 6, 1866, description of the Portland fire

Jonathan Morgan, 1869, letter requesting assistance from the city of Portland after the great fire of 1866

Anne Longfellow Pierce, to sister Mary, July 5, 1866 (courtesy of National Park Service, Longfellow historic site)

DIARIES

William Williis, entries of July and August 1866, Maine Historical Society files

CREDITS

All black-and-white fire pictures courtesy Maine Historic Preservation Commission.

Front cover picture, fire trail map, Brown letter courtesy Maine Historical Society.

Ann Longfellow letter courtesy of the Longfellow National Historic Site.

Bill Paxton painting courtesy Judie Percival.

CPSIA information can be obtained at www.ICGtesting.com
Printed in the USA
LVOW05s0904041214

417131LV00001B/118/P